Especially for kids and their families

# The Mini Page.
# BOOK OF STATES

Especially for kids and their families

# The Mini Page

# BOOK OF STATES

## by Betty Debnam

**Andrews and McMeel**
A Universal Press Syndicate Company
**Kansas City**

Library of Congress Cataloging-in-Publication Data

Debnam, Betty.
    The Mini page book of states/by Betty Debnam.
        p.      cm.
    Summary: One-page entries, arranged alphabetically, present
information about the history, geography, industries, and special
tourist attractions of the fifty states.
        ISBN 0-8362-4204-1 : $4.95
        1. United States—Miscellanea—Juvenile literature. [1. United
States.]      I. Title.

E156.D43 1988
973—dc19                                                    88-28694
                                                                CIP
                                                                 AC


First Printing, November 1988
Sixth Printing, June 1996

# CONTENTS

| | | | |
|---|---|---|---|
| Population by State | 7 | Missouri | 60 |
| United States Map | 8 | Montana | 62 |
| Alabama | 10 | Nebraska | 64 |
| Alaska | 12 | Nevada | 66 |
| Arizona | 14 | New Hampshire | 68 |
| Arkansas | 16 | New Jersey | 70 |
| California | 18 | New Mexico | 72 |
| Colorado | 20 | New York | 74 |
| Connecticut | 22 | North Carolina | 76 |
| Delaware | 24 | North Dakota | 78 |
| District of Columbia | 26 | Ohio | 80 |
| Florida | 28 | Oklahoma | 82 |
| Georgia | 30 | Oregon | 84 |
| Hawaii | 32 | Pennsylvania | 86 |
| Idaho | 34 | Rhode Island | 88 |
| Illinois | 36 | South Carolina | 90 |
| Indiana | 38 | South Dakota | 92 |
| Iowa | 40 | Tennessee | 94 |
| Kansas | 42 | Texas | 96 |
| Kentucky | 44 | Utah | 98 |
| Louisiana | 46 | Vermont | 100 |
| Maine | 48 | Virginia | 102 |
| Maryland | 50 | Washington | 104 |
| Massachusetts | 52 | West Virginia | 106 |
| Michigan | 54 | Wisconsin | 108 |
| Minnesota | 56 | Wyoming | 110 |
| Mississippi | 58 | | |

# POPULATION BY STATE

| | | | |
|---|---|---|---|
| Alabama | 4,053,000 | Missouri | 5,066,000 |
| Alaska | 534,000 | Montana | 819,000 |
| Arizona | 3,317,000 | Nebraska | 1,598,000 |
| Arkansas | 2,372,000 | Nevada | 963,000 |
| California | 26,981,000 | New Hampshire | 1,027,000 |
| Colorado | 3,267,000 | New Jersey | 7,620,000 |
| Connecticut | 3,189,000 | New Mexico | 1,479,000 |
| Delaware | 633,000 | New York | 17,772,000 |
| District of | | North Carolina | 6,331,000 |
| Columbia | 626,000 | North Dakota | 679,000 |
| Florida | 11,675,000 | Ohio | 10,752,000 |
| Georgia | 5,975,000 | Oklahoma | 3,305,000 |
| Hawaii | 1,062,000 | Oregon | 2,698,000 |
| Idaho | 1,003,000 | Pennsylvania | 11,889,000 |
| Illinois | 11,553,000 | Rhode Island | 975,000 |
| Indiana | 5,504,000 | South Carolina | 3,378,000 |
| Iowa | 2,851,000 | South Dakota | 708,000 |
| Kansas | 2,461,000 | Tennessee | 4,803,000 |
| Kentucky | 3,728,000 | Texas | 16,682,000 |
| Louisiana | 4,501,000 | Utah | 1,665,000 |
| Maine | 1,174,000 | Vermont | 541,000 |
| Maryland | 4,463,000 | Virginia | 5,787,000 |
| Massachusetts | 5,832,000 | Washington | 4,463,000 |
| Michigan | 9,145,000 | West Virginia | 1,919,000 |
| Minnesota | 4,214,000 | Wisconsin | 4,785,000 |
| Mississippi | 2,625,000 | Wyoming | 507,000 |

Population figures are based on 1986 estimates by the
U.S. Bureau of the Census, Commerce Department.

Washington

Oregon

Montana

North Dakota

Idaho

South Dakota

Wyoming

Nevada

Nebraska

Utah

Colorado

California

Kansas

Arizona

New Mexico

Oklahoma

Texas

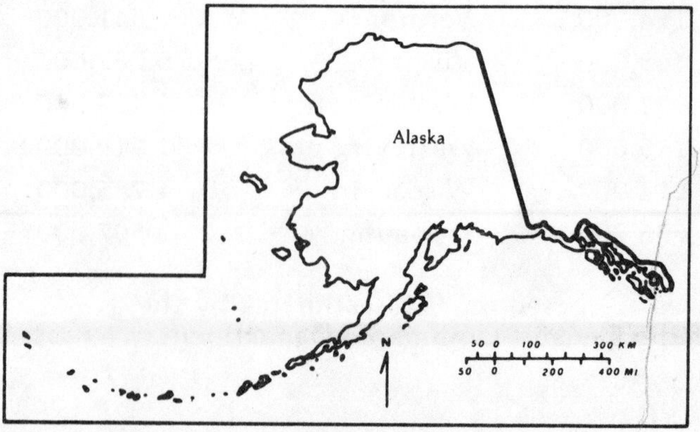

Alaska

N

50 0    100      300 KM
50 0       200      400 MI

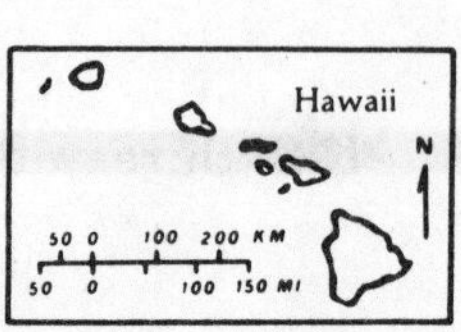

Hawaii

N

50 0   100 200 KM
50 0    100 150 MI

8

Maine

Vermont

Michigan

Minnesota

New Hampshire

Massachusetts

Rhode Island

Connecticut

New York

Wisconsin

Pennsylvania

Iowa

New Jersey

Ohio

Delaware

Indiana

District of Columbia

Illinois

West Virginia

Maryland

Virginia

Missouri

Kentucky

North Carolina

Tennessee

South Carolina

Arkansas

Alabama

Georgia

Mississippi

Louisiana

Florida

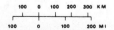

100    0    100   200   300 KM

100    0    100    200 MI

Map by Lewis A. Armstrong from base map of the U.S. Geological Survey
1:5,000,000 scale map of the United States.

# ALABAMA

**Capital:** Montgomery

**State name:** comes from the name of an Indian tribe that once lived in the region.

**Nickname:** The Heart of Dixie

## Facts About Alabama

Alabama played a big part in the Civil War. Jefferson Davis was inaugurated as president of the Confederacy in Montgomery which was the first capital of the Confederacy.

The nation's first electric trolley streetcar began in Montgomery. Scientist George Washington Carver did research at Tuskegee Institute.

Manufacturing is the biggest industry. Some chief manufactured goods are paper products, textiles, clothing, chemicals, and rubber and plastic products.

The mining of coal, petroleum, and bauxite is important.

Farmers raise a lot of beef cattle and poultry. Crops grown include soybeans, cotton, corn, peanuts, pecans, and wheat.

Seafood is a big industry on the coast. Fishermen catch a lot of shrimp, oysters, and red snapper.

The state is the home of the world's largest space exhibit, the Alabama Space and Rocket Center in Huntsville.

Alabama's coast is along the Gulf of Mexico. There are also hills, rolling plains, rivers, pine forests, swamps, and bayous.

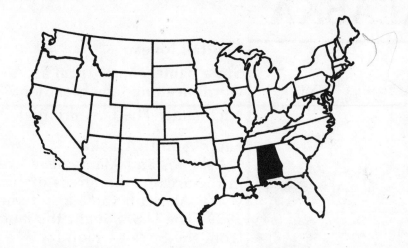

**Entered union:** December 14, 1819
(22nd state)

**Motto:** *Audemus jura nostra defendere*
(We dare defend our rights)

**Square miles:** 51,609

**Abbreviations:** Ala. (traditional)
AL (postal)

**State bird:** yellowhammer

**State flower:** camellia

**State tree:** Southern pine

**Flag:** a red cross on a
white field

11

# ALASKA

**Capital:** Juneau

**State name:** comes from an Aleut word meaning "the great land."

**Nickname:** The Last Frontier

## Facts About Alaska

Eskimos and Aleuts have lived in the area for hundreds of years. Alaska became a state in 1959. The U.S. bought the land from the Soviet Union for $7,200,000 in 1867.

The mining of oil, natural gas, gold, sand and gravel, stone, silver, platinum, coal, lead, zinc, and copper are other big industries.

Alaska makes more money from fishing than any state. Seafood caught include salmon, crab, halibut, and sea herring.

Tourism is another important industry. People come to see the beautiful scenery.

Our largest state has mountains, lowlands, many islands, and the longest coastline of any state. It also has a variety of climates with temperatures as high as 100 degrees in the summer to minus 80 degrees in the winter. Some parts have lots of rain. The highest peak in the U.S. is Mount McKinley at 20,320 feet. There are also thousands of lakes and lots of rivers.

Juneau covers 3,108 square miles, making it the largest city in area in the U.S. The state's westernmost mainland point is only 51 miles from the Soviet Union. The northernmost point of the U.S. is at Point Barrow.

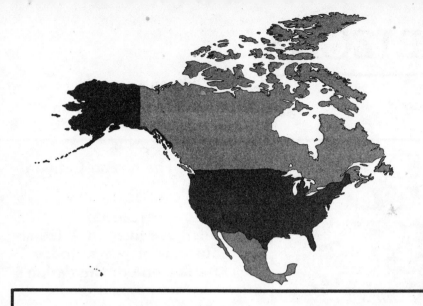

Entered union: January 3, 1959
(49th state)

Motto: North to the future

Square miles: 586,412

Abbreviation: AK

State bird: willow ptarmigan

State flower: forget-me-not

State tree: Sitka spruce

Flag: seven gold stars in the Big Dipper shape. An eighth star in the corner stands for the state's northern location

# ARIZONA

**Capital:** Phoenix

**State name:** comes from an Indian word that some believe means "small spring."

**Nickname:** The Grand Canyon State

## Facts About Arizona

Indians have lived in Arizona for thousands of years. Today, the state has one of the nation's largest Indian populations.

The planet Pluto was discovered from the Lowell Observatory in Flagstaff in 1930.

In the 1500s, Spaniards came to the area looking for gold. Today, Arizona leads the nation in the production of copper. Mining for gold, coal, silver, lead, and sand and gravel is a big industry.

Much of the land is irrigated so that crops such as cotton, hay, lettuce, apples, and citrus fruits can be grown. Farmers also raise sheep and beef cattle.

Electrical machinery, transportation equipment, and computers are made in Arizona.

Tourists come to visit the Grand Canyon, the Petrified Forest, the Painted Desert, and ghost towns. Another popular site is Four Corners where the states Arizona, New Mexico, Colorado, and Utah meet.

Arizona is a scenic state with deserts, mountains, forests, deep canyons, and plateaus. Cactus and lizards are found in the desert. The government owns or controls over 70 percent of the land.

Entered union: February 14, 1912
(48th state)

Motto: *Ditat Deus*
(God enriches)

Square miles: 113,909

Abbreviations: Ariz. (traditional)
AZ (postal)

**State bird:** cactus wren

**State tree:** paloverde

**State flower:** blossom of the saguaro
cactus

**Flag:** a copper-colored
star in the center with
red-and-gold stripes at
the top and a blue bottom

# ARKANSAS

**Capital:** Little Rock

**State name:** comes from an Indian word meaning "downstream people."

**Nickname:** The Land of Opportunity

## Facts About Arkansas

Arkansas was explored by de Soto in 1541. The U.S. bought the land in 1803 as part of the Louisiana Purchase.

Farming is a big source of income. The state is a leader in raising poultry and rice and producing eggs. Other crops grown include soybeans, cotton, wheat, tomatoes, and watermelons.

Manufacturing is also an important industry. This includes food products such as animal feed, poultry, grain, and milk, microwave ovens, refrigerators, aluminum products, televisions, and lumber and wood products such as cabinets and plywood.

Mining of bauxite, oil, bromine, and natural gas is a big industry.

The Crater of Diamonds State Park, once a diamond mine, is now the only diamond-hunting field in North America.

Arkansas is popular with tourists. There are lakes for fishing and boating. Springs are big attractions because many people believe their waters cure some illnesses. Hot Springs was set aside as the first federal reservation in 1832. It is now a health resort.

Forests cover much of the state. There are also mountains, valleys, and flatland. The Mississippi River is the eastern border.

Entered union: June 15, 1836
(25th state)

Motto: *Regnat populus*
(The people rule)

Square miles: 53,104

Abbreviations: Ark. (traditional)
AR (postal)

State bird: mockingbird

State flower: apple blossom

State tree: pine

Flag: a diamond on a red background

# CALIFORNIA

**Capital:** Sacramento

**State name:** probably named by Spanish explorers after a treasure island in a Spanish story.

**Nickname:** The Golden State

## Facts About California

California was explored by the Spanish and English in the 1500s. A gold rush in the 1800s brought many settlers to the area.

The state leads all others in manufacturing. Transportation and electronic equipment are produced there. Food processing is also big. California leads the nation in the production of aircraft and space equipment.

California is also the top farm state. It is first in several agricultural products, including asparagus, broccoli, lettuce, tomatoes, and many other crops. Farmers also raise peaches, cotton, grapes, flowers, citrus fruit, almonds, cattle, and sheep.

California is richer in minerals than any other state. Oil is the most important product mined.

Fishing is a big industry.

Most U.S. movie and TV studios are located in the state.

There are beaches along the Pacific Ocean on the west, mountains in the east, deserts in the southeast, and giant redwood forests in the northwest. The state is known for its warm, sunny weather during the summer and its mild winters. Many sports, especially water sports, are popular.

**Entered union:** September 9, 1850
(31st state)

**Motto:** *Eureka*
(I have found it)

**Square miles:** 158,693

**Abbreviations:** Cal. (traditional)
CA (postal)

**State bird:** California valley quail    **State tree:** California redwood
**State flower:** golden poppy

**Flag:** grizzly bear on a
white background

# COLORADO

**Capital:** Denver

**State name:** comes from the Spanish word meaning "colored red."

**Nickname:** The Centennial State

## Facts About Colorado

Colorado was the home of many Indian tribes in its early days. There were few settlements until the Gold Rush in the late 1850s.

Manufacturing is a leading industry. Some manufactured goods include food products, photographic and medical instruments, non-electric machinery, and books and magazines.

Farming is also important. Some crops are potatoes, sugar beets, wheat, corn, hay, cantaloupes, and flowers. Livestock and dairy products are also important.

The state has a large mining industry. Products include uranium, silver, gold, lead, and coal. The most valuable mineral is petroleum.

Colorado is very popular with tourists. They visit the U.S. Mint in Denver, the U.S. Air Force Academy in Colorado Springs, and Rocky Mountain National Park. Tourists also come to ski at many popular ski resorts.

Colorado is known for its beautiful scenery. There are plateaus and mountains in the west and plains in the east. The Rocky Mountains in the middle contain some of the tallest mountains in the U.S.

**Entered union:** August 1, 1876
(38th state)

**Motto:** *Nil sine Numine*
(Nothing without Providence)

**Square miles:** 104,247

**Abbreviations:** Colo. (traditional)
CO (postal)

**State bird:** lark bunting          **State tree:** blue spruce
**State flower:** Rocky Mountain columbine

**Flag:** a red "C" on blue
and white stripes

# CONNECTICUT

**Capital:** Hartford

**State name:** comes from an Indian word meaning "on the long tidal river."

**Nickname:** The Constitution State

## Facts About Connecticut

Connecticut is a historic state. It was the home of many Indians. It played a big part in the Revolutionary War and was one of the original 13 colonies.

The state is the home of the nation's first law school and state prison. Also, the country's first submarine, steamboat, pay phone, sewing machine, lollipop, assembly line, revolver, bicycle, hamburger, and Frisbee were from there.

Manufacturing is an important industry. Products include helicopters, jet engines, submarines, pharmacy products, and machinery.

Many insurance companies are located there.

Farmers produce chickens, eggs, dairy products, and apples. There are also many vineyards.

Colonial villages and buildings and old whaling towns are popular tourist sites. The state is also known for its small white churches on village greens (public parks).

The Connecticut River divides the state in half. There are lowlands in the center and mountains in the northwest. There are also lakes and waterfalls. Long Island Sound is the southern border.

**Entered union:** January 9, 1788
  (5th state)

**Motto:** *Qui transtulit sustinet*
  (He who transplanted still sustains)

**Square miles:** 5,009

**Abbreviations:** Conn. (traditional)
  CT (postal)

**State bird:** robin                    **State tree:** white oak

**State flower:** mountain laurel

**Flag:** blue with a
grapevine symbol in the
middle

# DELAWARE

**Capital:** Dover

**State name:** named for Lord De La Warr, a former governor of Virginia.

**Nickname:** The First State

## Facts About Delaware

Delaware was the first state to ratify the Constitution. For this reason, it is always the leader in the presidential inaugural parade.

The nation's first Christmas seals were designed and sold in Wilmington in 1907.

Chemicals and chemical products are the main industry. Wilmington is called the "Chemical Capital of the World." Du Pont, one of the world's largest chemical companies, has its headquarters there. Most of its products are made other places. The company produces drugs, industrial chemicals, fabrics, plastics, paint, and golf balls.

Other important industries include fruit packing, food canning, and producing instruments. Auto assembly plants are also important.

The state is a big poultry producer. Yearly, farmers raise about 300 broilers per person in the state.

The coastline is popular with tourists and fishermen.

Delaware is a tiny state. It is only about 100 miles long and 35 miles wide at its widest point. Most of the state is a flat plain except for hills and valleys in the north.

Entered union: December 7, 1787
(1st state)

Motto: Liberty and independence

Square miles: 2,057

Abbreviations: Del. (traditional)
DE (postal)

State bird: blue hen chicken    State tree: American holly
State flower: peach blossom

Flag: blue with a modified version of the state seal in the middle

25

# DISTRICT OF COLUMBIA

**Facts About Washington, D.C.**
Washington, D.C., was chosen to be the home of the U.S. government by George Washington in 1791. He hired a French engineer to plan the city. It replaced Philadelphia as the nation's capital in 1800.

Government is the city's main business. The White House, Capitol, Supreme Court, and FBI are located there. Thousands of people work for the government.

Many tourists visit Washington. People can tour the White House, Capitol, FBI Building, office buildings of congressmen and senators, Library of Congress, Department of Treasury, and other government buildings. Also popular are the Washington Monument and the Lincoln, Jefferson, and Vietnam Memorials.

The Smithsonian museums are especially popular. They contain over 75 million items, including the Wright Brothers' plane, the Hope Diamond, George Washington's false teeth, mummies, Dorothy's shoes from *The Wizard of Oz*, and the flag that inspired Francis Scott Key to write "The Star Spangled Banner."

Washington is a beautiful city on the Potomac River. It has about 150 parks and many old and historic buildings. In the spring, it is famous for the blooming Japanese cherry trees.

Washington is the only city in the U.S. that is not part of a state. It covers 68 square miles between Virginia and Maryland.

**Became U.S. capital:** December 1, 1800
**Motto:** *Justitia omnibus*
       (Justice to all)
**Square miles:** 68

**Flower:** American beauty rose          **Tree:** Scarlet oak

**Flag:** three stars and two red
bars on a white background

# FLORIDA

**Capital:** Tallahassee

**State name:** comes from the Spanish word meaning "full of flowers."

**Nickname:** The Sunshine State

## Facts About Florida

Ponce de Leon came to Florida in 1513 looking for the Fountain of Youth. He claimed the land for Spain. In 1819 the United States acquired Florida from Spain.

Florida is the home of the first U.S. air-training facility, the first commercial airline flight, and the oldest permanent European settlement in the United States, St. Augustine, founded in 1565.

Tourism is a big industry. The pleasant climate, beach resorts, and water sports attract people year-round. Popular sites include Walt Disney World, Epcot Center, Everglades National Park, and the Kennedy Space Center.

Florida grows more oranges and grapefruits than any state. Other crops include watermelons, limes, tangerines, and mangoes.

Food processing is a major industry. This includes producing jelly, citrus fruit products, and canned and frozen seafood.

Florida is a leading fishing state. This includes shrimp, scallops, and red snapper.

Florida is a peninsula about 460 miles long. The Gulf of Mexico is on the west and the Atlantic Ocean is on the east. Most of the land is level plains and swampland. The state has about 30,000 lakes.

**Entered union:** March 3, 1845
             (27th state)
**Motto:** In God we trust
**Square miles:** 58,560
**Abbreviations:** Fla. (traditional)
                    FL (postal)

**State bird:** mockingbird       **State tree:** cabbage palmetto
        **State flower:** orange blossom

**Flag:** the state seal on a
white background with
red diagonal stripes

# GEORGIA

**Capital:** Atlanta

**State name:** named after King George II of England.

**Nickname:** The Peach State

## Facts About Georgia

De Soto explored Georgia in 1540. The first settlement was made by the English in 1733. The state was the youngest of the original 13 colonies. Many Civil War battles were fought there.

The nation's first ice-making machine, cotton gin, Girl Scout troop, movie theater, and Coca-Cola were from Georgia.

Producing textiles is a large industry. Other important industries include car, truck, and boat manufacturing; food production such as peanut butter and cane syrup; chemicals; paper and wood products such as newsprint and railroad ties.

Georgia leads the nation in growing peanuts and pecans. It is also a big producer of chickens, cattle, pigs, tobacco, peaches, watermelons, and cotton.

The nation's first gold rush took place in Georgia in 1828. The state used to be a major producer of gold. Today, it produces a lot of clay, marble, and granite.

Shrimp is an important seafood product.

The state has mountains in the north. There are also hills, plains, and forests.

**Entered union:** January 2, 1788
(4th state)
**Motto:** Wisdom, justice, and moderation
**Square miles:** 58,876
**Abbreviations:** Ga. (traditional)
GA (postal)

**State bird:** brown thrasher **State tree:** live oak
**State flower:** Cherokee rose

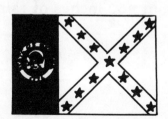

**Flag:** the state seal and
the Confederate flag

# HAWAII

**Capital:** Honolulu

**State name:** origin uncertain.

**Nickname:** The Aloha State

## Facts About Hawaii

Hawaii was originally settled by the Polynesians (pol-uh-nee-zhuns), who were people from other Pacific islands. The islands were later explored by Captain James Cook in 1778. Hawaii is our youngest state.

Most of the state's income comes from tourists. People come for the beautiful scenery, weather, and beaches. The state is famous for its many water sports.

Food processing is an important manufacturing activity. Some leading crops are sugar cane and pineapples. Hawaii is the only state in the U.S. that grows coffee.

The largest permanent military establishment in the Pacific is located in Hawaii.

Hawaii is a beautiful state with deep-blue water, palm trees, waterfalls, and flowers. It is made up of 132 islands and is the only state in the U.S. that does not lie on the mainland of North America. The state has many volcanoes, including Mauna Loa, the largest in the world. The wettest place in the world is Mount Waialeale on the island of Kauai. It gets about 460 inches of rain a year.

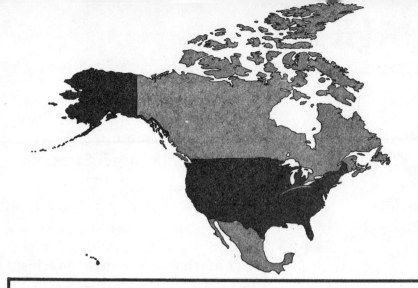

**Entered union:** August 21, 1959
  (50th state)

**Motto:** The life of the land is perpetuated in
  righteousness

**Square miles:** 6,450

**Abbreviation:** HI

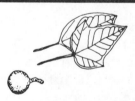

**State bird:** nene (nay-nay)
**State flower:** hibiscus
**State tree:** live oak

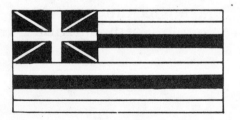

**Flag:** white, red, and blue
with stripes symbolizing
the eight main islands in
the Hawaiian chain, and
the English Union Jack in
the upper-left corner

# IDAHO

**Capital:** Boise

**State name:** comes from the Shoshone Indian word for "sun coming down mountain."

**Nickname:** The Gem State

## Facts About Idaho

Indians lived in Idaho thousands of years ago. Lewis and Clark explored the area in 1805. The first settlers were missionaries and fur traders and trappers.

Agriculture is an important industry. Idaho leads the nation in growing potatoes. Other crops grown include sugar beets, apples, hay, wheat, peas, and lentils. Farmers also raise cattle and sheep.

Lumber and wood production is another important industry.

Mining is also a large industry. Idaho leads the nation in silver production. Lead, copper, zinc, phosphate rock, and gold are also mined. The state was the site of a gold rush in the 1860s. Many mining towns from that era can still be seen today.

Idaho's beautiful scenery and snow sports such as skiing are popular with tourists. Part of Yellowstone National Park lies in the state.

The land includes mountains, lakes, forests, rivers, and waterfalls. Hell's Canyon, through which the Snake River flows, is the deepest canyon in North America.

**Entered union:** July 3, 1890
             (43rd state)
**Motto:** *Esto perpetua*
       (It is perpetual)
**Square miles:** 83,557
**Abbreviation:** ID

**State bird:** mountain bluebird          **State tree:** Western white pine
                    **State flower:** syringa

**Flag:** the state seal on a
blue background

# ILLINOIS

**Capital:** Springfield

**State name:** comes from the Indian word "Illiniwek," meaning "superior men."

**Nickname:** Land of Lincoln

## Facts About Illinois

Illinois was the home of many Indian tribes. Fur trading was important in the late 1600s.

The nation's first railroad sleeping car came from the state.

Chicago, one of the largest cities in the country, is located on Lake Michigan.

Manufacturing is the main industry. Products include diesel engines, televisions, farm machinery, tools, and steel.

Food processing is also important. The state ranks first in candy and in corn products such as syrup and starch. Butter and cheese are also made there. It is the leader in making Swiss cheese.

Printing and publishing are also big.

Illinois' rich farmland produces more soybeans than any state. Other crops include corn, popcorn, oats, wheat, barley, apples, and cabbage. Farmers also raise cattle and hogs.

The state is first in the U.S. in the production of soft coal. Oil is also important.

The land is mostly plains, but there are also hills and many lakes and rivers.

**Entered union:** December 3, 1818
(21st state)
**Motto:** State sovereignty, national union
**Square miles:** 56,400
**Abbreviations:** Ill. (traditional)
IL (postal)

**State bird:** cardinal

**State flower:** native violet

**State tree:** white oak

**Flag:** an adaptation of the state seal on a white background

# INDIANA

**Capital:** Indianapolis

**State name:** means "the land of Indians."

**Nickname:** The Hoosier State

## Facts About Indiana

La Salle explored Indiana in the 1600s. The first permanent settlement, Vincennes, was established by the French in the early 1700s.

The first Raggedy Ann doll was made in Indianapolis in 1914. The first professional baseball game was played in Fort Wayne in 1871.

Manufacturing is an important industry. Many steel mills and oil refineries are located there. Major products are record players, musical instruments, radios, televisions, car parts, and aircraft engines.

Farmers grow corn, soybeans, popcorn, and wheat. Hogs are a major livestock crop.

The mining of coal and building limestone is important.

The Indianapolis 500, a 500-mile car race, probably attracts more people than any other sports event in the nation.

Indiana is popular with tourists. There are sand dunes near Lake Michigan and many streams and lakes for boating and fishing. There are also forests, plains, and rolling hills. The Wyandotte Cave is one of largest caves in the country.

**Entered union:** December 11, 1816
(19th state)

**Motto:** Crossroads of America

**Square miles:** 36,291

**Abbreviations:** Ind. (traditional)
IN (postal)

**State bird:** cardinal

**State flower:** peony

**State tree:** tulip tree

**Flag:** 19 gold stars and a gold torch on a blue background

# IOWA

**Capital:** Des Moines

**State name:** comes from the Indian word for "this is the place."

**Nickname:** The Hawkeye State

## Facts About Iowa

Indians lived in Iowa at least 12,000 years ago. French explorers Marquette and Joliet explored the area in the late 1600s. It was later sold to the United States as part of the Louisiana Purchase.

Iowa is a leading state in the percentage of people who read and write.

Iowa is one of the greatest farming states. Farms cover over 90 percent of the land. Farmers raise corn, soybeans, oats, hay, apples, onions, green beans, hogs, and cattle. Dairy products are also important.

Manufacturing is big in the state. Farm equipment, washers, dryers, and chemicals are made there.

Food processing is another big industry. This includes meat packing and the production of popcorn, breakfast cereals, and corn oil.

The land is mostly plains with rolling hills. In the northeast there are rugged hills and cliffs. The Mississippi River forms the eastern border. The Missouri River is on the west.

**Entered union:** December 28, 1846
(29th state)

**Motto:** Our liberties we prize and our rights
we will maintain

**Square miles:** 56,290

**Abbreviation:** IA

**State bird:** Eastern goldfinch

**State flower:** wild rose

**State tree:** oak

**Flag:** red, white, and blue
stripes, with a picture of
an eagle in the middle

# KANSAS

**Capital:** Topeka

**State name:** an Indian word meaning "people of the south wind."

**Nickname:** The Sunflower State

## Facts About Kansas

Spanish explorer Coronado explored parts of Kansas in the 1500s. The state was sold to the United States as part of the Louisiana Purchase in 1803.

Agriculture is an important industry. The state is first in wheat and milo (a type of grain). Other crops are corn, sorghum, hay, popcorn, and sugar beets. Farmers also raise beef cattle and hogs.

Kansas is a world leader in the production of aircraft. Over half the nation's light airplanes are built in the Wichita area.

Farm equipment, railroad cars, and rubber tires are also made in the state.

Kansas is among the leading mineral-producing states, with petroleum, natural gas, propane, helium, and salt.

Among the places tourists come to visit are Dodge City, a famous cowtown once known as the Cowboy Capital of the World, and a rebuilt cabin near Independence where Laura Ingalls Wilder lived as a child.

Kansas has cold winters and warm summers. Winds move easily across the plains and the weather can change quickly.

There are hills and forests in the east and open plains in the west.

**Entered union:** January 29, 1861
(34th state)

**Motto:** *Ad astra per aspera*
(To the stars through difficulties)

**Square miles:** 82,264

**Abbreviations:** Kans. (traditional)
KS (postal)

**State bird:** meadowlark

**State flower:** sunflower

**State tree:** cottonwood

**Flag:** blue, with the state
seal in the middle

# KENTUCKY

**Capital:** Frankfort

**State name:** comes from an Indian word "Kah-ten-tah-teh" meaning "land of tomorrow" or "meadowland."

**Nickname:** The Bluegrass State

## Facts About Kentucky

Daniel Boone explored the area in the 1700s. The first settlers lived in log cabins. Abraham Lincoln was born in Kentucky. Several Civil War battles were fought there.

Farming is an important industry. The state produces a lot of tobacco. Farmers also raise beef cattle, corn, wheat, soybeans, hay, and apples.

Kentucky leads the nation in coal production.

Trucks, cigarettes, chemicals, and clothing are all made in the state.

Many thoroughbred horse farms are located in Kentucky. The Kentucky Derby, a famous horse race, is held at Churchill Downs in Louisville.

Kentucky is the home of Fort Knox where U.S. government gold is kept.

Mammoth Cave National Park, which includes the world's longest known cave system, is a popular site.

The northern border is the Ohio River. The Appalachian Mountains are in the east. These turn to rolling flatlands with coal mining valleys in the northwest.

**Entered union:** June 1, 1792
 (15th state)
**Motto:** United we stand, divided we fall
**Square miles:** 40,409
**Abbreviations:** Ky. (traditional)
 KY (postal)

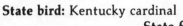

**State bird:** Kentucky cardinal  **State tree:** Kentucky coffee tree
 **State flower:** goldenrod

**Flag:** blue, with the state seal in the middle

# LOUISIANA

**Capital:** Baton Rouge

**State name:** named after King Louis XIV of France.

**Nickname:** The Pelican State

## Facts About Louisiana

Louisiana was explored by La Salle in 1682. The area was later sold to the U.S. as part of the Louisiana Purchase.

Louisiana is one of the leading states in the production of natural gas and petroleum. Salt mining is also important.

The state manufactures chemicals and petroleum products. Food processing, including meat-packing and sugar and rice production, is also big.

Louisiana is the leading shrimp state. Other catches include oysters, crawfish, and red snapper.

The state is also number one in furs. This includes mink, muskrat, otter, and beaver.

Farmers raise rice, sugar cane, sweet potatoes, cotton, soybeans, and beef cattle.

New Orleans, located where the Mississippi River flows into the Gulf of Mexico, is one of the busiest ports in the world. Mardi Gras, a colorful festival held in the French Quarter of New Orleans each year, attracts many tourists.

The Mississippi River, once famous for paddle-wheel steamboats, flows through the state. The river is so large that ocean ships can travel over 200 miles upriver to Baton Rouge.

Entered union: April 30, 1812
(18th state)

Motto: Union, justice, and confidence

Square miles: 48,523

Abbreviations: La. (traditional)
LA (postal)

**State bird:** brown pelican

**State flower:** magnolia

**State tree:** bald cypress

**Flag:** blue with a pelican on it

# MAINE

**Capital:** Augusta

**State name:** probably came from "mainland." English settlers used "the main" to mean the mainland and not an island.

**Nickname:** The Pine Tree State

## Facts About Maine

Vikings probably visited Maine around the year 1000. The English established many permanent settlements in the 1600s.

Maine is a leading seafood state. It ranks first in the number of lobsters caught and sardines packed each year. Other important seafood catches include clams, scallops, shrimp, and flounder.

Paper products and lumber are the main manufactured goods. The state is the leader in toothpicks and has some of the world's largest newsprint factories.

The first boat built in America was built in Maine in 1607. Today, the state is the home of Bath Iron Works, one of the nation's largest shipbuilders.

The freezing and canning of blueberries, chickens, and french-fried potatoes is important.

Farmers raise potatoes, oats, apples, chickens, and cattle.

Sand, gravel, and zinc are all mined in the state.

Maine is famous for its beautiful rocky coastline and many lighthouses. There are also lakes, rivers, and mountains. Forests cover about 90 percent of the land. West Quoddy Head is the easternmost point in the U.S.

**Entered union:** March 15, 1820
(23rd state)
**Motto:** *Dirigo*
(I direct)
**Square miles:** 33,215
**Abbreviation:** ME

**State bird:** chickadee          **State tree:** Eastern white pine
**State flower:** white pinecone and tassel

**Flag:** blue, with the state
seal in the middle

# MARYLAND

**Capital:** Annapolis

**State name:** comes from Queen Henrietta Maria, the wife of King Charles I of England.

**Nickname:** The Old Line State

## Facts About Maryland

Maryland was explored by the English in the 1600s. One of the first settlements was St. Mary's City established by colonists sent by Lord Baltimore in 1634.

The U.S. Naval Academy is in Annapolis. This city was the nation's capital from 1783 to 1784. The statehouse is the oldest still in use.

The bombardment of Fort McHenry in Baltimore Harbor inspired Francis Scott Key to write "The Star-Spangled Banner."

The first ship for the U.S. Navy, the *USS Constellation*, was built in Baltimore in 1797. The telegraph message Samuel Morse sent from Baltimore to Washington, D.C., in 1844 was the first one ever sent.

Manufacturing is an important industry. Products include appliances, electronics such as computers, and transportation equipment such as automobiles.

Farmers raise tobacco, corn, apples, and broiler chickens.

Seafood packing is an important industry. The state harvests a lot of oysters and blue crabs.

Chesapeake Bay, the largest in the nation, divides the state in half. The eastern half is low and flat. The western half has plateaus, hills, and mountains.

**Entered union:** April 28, 1788
(7th state)

**Motto:** *Fatti maschi, parole femine*
(Manly deeds, womanly words)

**Square miles:** 10,577

**Abbreviations:** Md. (traditional)
MD (postal)

**State bird:** Baltimore oriole          **State tree:** white oak
**State flower:** black-eyed susan

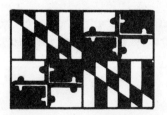

**Flag:** the coat of arms of
the Lords Baltimore who
founded Maryland

# MASSACHUSETTS

**Capital:** Boston

**State name:** named for the Massachusetts Indian tribe, which lived there when the Pilgrims arrived.

**Nickname:** The Bay State

## Facts About Massachusetts

The state played a big part in American history. The Pilgrims landed there in 1620 and celebrated the first Thanksgiving one year later. The Revolutionary War started at Lexington and Concord. The state was also the site of the Boston Tea Party and Paul Revere's ride.

America's first university (Harvard), post office, public school, newspaper, Christmas card, subway system, and computer were started or invented in the state.

Boston is also known as an important center for scientific research.

Important farm products are milk, poultry, vegetables, and livestock. The state is first in growing cranberries.

Manufacturing is important. Products include office machines, aircraft engines, lamps, televisions, radios, instruments used for scientific research, and leather products such as shoes.

Printing and publishing are big businesses.

Fishing, especially for cod and scallops, is a big industry.

The eastern coastline has many bays and islands. The western part has hills and valleys.

**Entered union:** February 6, 1788
(6th state)

**Motto:** *Ense petit placidam sub libertate quietem*
(By the sword we seek peace, but
peace only under liberty)

**Square miles:** 8,257

**Abbreviations:** Mass. (traditional)
MA (postal)

**State bird:** chickadee                    **State tree:** American elm
          **State flower:** mayflower

**Flag:** coat of arms on a
white background

# MICHIGAN

**Capital:** Lansing

**State name:** comes from the Indian word "Michigama" which means "big water."

**Nickname:** The Wolverine State

## Facts About Michigan

Many Indians lived in Michigan. During the 1600s, Marquette and Joliet explored the area.

Michigan is a leader in the production of automobile parts and engines, truck trailers, sporting equipment, refrigerators, and hardware.

Agriculture is an important industry. The state is the world's leading grower of navy beans. Farmers also raise apples, grapes, plums, cherries, strawberries, asparagus, mushrooms, celery, blueberries, and livestock. Dairy products are also important.

Battle Creek produces more breakfast cereal than any place in the country.

Michigan is second in the nation in producing iron ore.

Detroit is called the automobile capital of the world. It leads the nation in producing cars and trucks.

The state has more inland water than any state. People are never more than six miles from a lake or stream. The state borders on four Great Lakes. Forests cover over half the state.

**Entered union:** January 26, 1837
(26th state)

**Motto:** *Si quaeris peninsulam amoenam circumspice*
(If you seek a pleasant peninsula, look about you)

**Square miles:** 58,216

**Abbreviations:** Mich. (traditional)
MI (postal)

**State bird:** robin

**State flower:** apple blossom

**State tree:** Eastern white pine

**Flag:** blue, with the state seal on it

# MINNESOTA

**Capital:** St. Paul

**State name:** comes from an Indian word meaning "sky-colored water."

**Nickname:** The Gopher State

## Facts About Minnesota

Many people believe the Vikings visited Minnesota in the 14th century. Fur traders, miners, and lumberjacks were also attracted to the area.

Farming is a major industry. The state is a leader in turkeys, oats, soybeans, and corn. Farmers also raise potatoes, sugar beets, chickens, hogs, and eggs.

Printing and publishing are important.

Food processing, especially milk, butter, cheese, and flour, is also big. Meat packing and vegetable canning are also done there.

Iron ore mining is a major industry.

Making electronics, such as computers, and wood products, such as window frames, are important.

Many people come to hunt, fish, and enjoy winter sports such as sledding, skiing, and ice skating. The state has over 15,000 lakes.

The Mississippi River has its source in Minnesota. Years ago, it was the number one route for steamboats and logs. The state's two largest cities, Minneapolis and St. Paul, have grown up side-by-side on the Mississippi. Forests cover much of the land.

Entered union: May 11, 1858
(32nd state)

Motto: *L'Etoile du Nord*
(The star of the North)

Square miles: 84,068

Abbreviations: Minn. (traditional),
MN (postal)

State bird: common loon

State tree: red pine

State flower: lady's-slipper

Flag: blue, with a white circle that says, "The Star of the North"

# MISSISSIPPI

**Capital:** Jackson

**State name:** Named after the Mississippi River.

**Nickname:** The Magnolia State

## Facts About Mississippi

Indians were the first people to live in the area. Hernando de Soto explored it while looking for gold in the 1500s. Many Civil War battles, including Vicksburg, were fought there.

The state is the home of America's first PTA, 4-H Club, state college for women, bottled Coca-Cola, and nuclear submarine.

Manufacturing is the largest industry. Products include ships, parts for cars and airplanes, motors, and clothing.

Oil and gas production is another important industry.

Forests cover over half the land. The state leads all others in the number of tree farms. Wood products such as mobile homes, plywood, and furniture are made there.

Many crops are grown because of the fertile soil and warm climate. These include rice, soybeans, cotton, peanuts, and sweet potatoes. Farmers also raise cattle and broilers.

The state is the largest producer of catfish. Shrimping is also important.

Tourists visit because of the pleasant weather, coastal resorts, and historical sites such as Civil War plantations.

The Gulf of Mexico forms part of the southern border and the Mississippi River is on the west.

**Entered union:** December 10, 1817
(20th state)

**Motto:** *Virtute et armis*
(By valor and arms)

**Square miles:** 47,716

**Abbreviations:** Miss. (traditional)
MS (postal)

**State bird:** mockingbird          **State tree:** Southern magnolia
                    **State flower:** magnolia

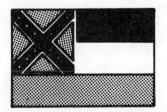

**Flag:** three stripes of red, white, and blue, with the Confederate Army flag in the upper left corner

# MISSOURI

**Capital:** Jefferson City

**State name:** comes from the Missouri River.

**Nickname:** The Show-Me State

## Facts About Missouri

The first settlers were French fur trappers and traders along the Mississippi River.

America's first railroad postal car, public kindergarten, and the Pony Express were started here. The ice cream cone and hot dog were invented at the 1904 World's Fair in St. Louis.

Manufacturing is a big industry. Products include airplanes, automobiles, railroad cars, electronics, and food products such as potato chips and country hams.

Missouri is a big agricultural state. Farmers raise corn, cotton, soybeans, wheat, apples, watermelons, strawberries, popcorn, hogs, turkeys, cattle, and chickens. It is also a leading grower of Christmas trees.

The Gateway Arch, the tallest national monument built in the U.S., is in St. Louis.

Missouri is known for its beautiful scenery. There are many caves, springs, and wildflowers.

The Mississippi River marks the eastern border. The Missouri River runs east and west through the state.

**Entered union:** August 10, 1821
(24th state)

**Motto:** *Salus populi suprema lex esto*
(The welfare of the people shall be
the supreme law)

**Square miles:** 69,686

**Abbreviations:** Mo. (traditional)
MO (postal)

**State bird:** bluebird

**State flower:** hawthorn

**State tree:** flowering dogwood

**Flag:** three bands of red,
white, and blue, with the
state seal in the middle

# MONTANA

**Capital:** Helena

**State name:** comes from the Latin word for "mountains."

**Nickname:** The Treasure State

## Facts About Montana

Montana has been the home of many Indian tribes for hundreds of years. Custer's Last Stand, near the Little Bighorn River, was a famous battle. Lewis and Clark explored the area in 1805 and 1806. A gold rush in 1862 and cattle ranching brought settlers to the state.

Agriculture is the state's leading source of income. This includes livestock such as cattle, hogs, and sheep, and products such as eggs, wool, and milk. The major crops are wheat, barley, sugar beets, and hay.

Mining is the second biggest industry. Petroleum, coal, copper, gold, silver, and zinc are found here.

Manufacturing is a big industry. Food products such as flour and sugar are made. Also important are lumber and wood products such as plywood, paper, and Christmas trees. Eureka is known as the "Christmas Tree Capital of the World."

Montana is a large state known for its beauty and untouched land. There are mountains and valleys in the west and plains in the east. Tourists come to ski and visit Glacier National Park and Yellowstone Park.

**Entered union:** November 8, 1889
(41st state)

**Motto:** *Oro y plata*
(Gold and silver)

**Square miles:** 147,138

**Abbreviations:** Mont. (traditional)
MT (postal)

**State bird:** Western meadowlark    **State tree:** ponderosa pine
**State flower:** bitterroot

**Flag:** the state seal on a
blue background

# NEBRASKA

**Capital:** Lincoln

**State name:** comes from the Indian word meaning "flat water."

**Nickname:** The Cornhusker State

## Facts About Nebraska

Indians have lived in Nebraska for at least 10,000 years. Today, there are three reservations. The development of railroads and the Homestead Act of 1862, which gave free land to settlers, helped populate, or settle, the area.

Nebraska was the site of the first rodeo, Buffalo Bill's Wild West Show, in 1883. The first Arbor Day was celebrated there in 1872. The largest mammoth fossil ever found was discovered near North Platte.

Agriculture is the state's leading source of income. Corn is the leading crop; wheat, rye, oats, and potatoes are also grown. The state ranks first in producing popcorn, great northern beans, and wild hay. Cattle ranching is also important.

Food processing is the leading industry, especially meat, flour, dairy, and vegetable products. The production of farm equipment, mobile homes, chemicals, car parts, and medical instruments are other important industries.

Nebraska has hills in the west and east while the central part is mostly flat. Nebraska National Forest is the largest man-made forest in the country.

Entered union: March 1, 1867
(37th state)
Motto: Equality before the law
Square miles: 77,227
Abbreviations: Nebr. (traditional)
NE (postal)

State bird: Western meadowlark
State flower: goldenrod

State tree: cottonwood

Flag: the state seal on a blue background

# NEVADA

**Capital:** Carson City

**State name:** comes from the Spanish word meaning "snow-clad."

**Nickname:** The Silver State

## Facts About Nevada

Most of Nevada was unexplored and unsettled until a rich deposit of silver was found in 1859. The discovery, called the Comstock Lode, brought thousands of miners to the area to "strike it rich."

Tourism is the state's leading industry. People come to gamble and enjoy the nightlife in Las Vegas, the largest city, and Reno. Nevada is one of the few areas in the country where gambling is legal. Skiing at Lake Tahoe is also popular. Ghost towns, rodeos, trout fishing, and deer hunting also attract tourists. Hoover Dam near Las Vegas is a popular site.

Raising cattle and sheep is the leading livestock industry. Because Nevada is dry, much of the land is irrigated so crops such as alfalfa, hay, potatoes, melons, wheat, oats, and cotton can be grown.

Mining was very big in the 1800s and is still an important industry today. Gold and silver are the most valuable minerals. Copper, lead, zinc, mercury, sand, and gravel are also mined.

Nevada's land is mostly mountains, desert, and broad valleys. A very dry state, it gets less rainfall than any other.

**Entered union:** October 31, 1864
(36th state)
**Motto:** All for our country
**Square miles:** 110,540
**Abbreviations:** Nev. (traditional)
NV (postal)

**State bird:** mountain bluebird          **State tree:** single-leaf piñon
**State flower:** sagebrush

**Flag:** blue, with the
words "Battle Born" in
the upper left corner

# NEW HAMPSHIRE

**Capital:** Concord

**State name:** named for Hampshire County in England.

**Nickname:** The Granite State

## Facts About New Hampshire

In 1776, New Hampshire became the first state to set up a government independent of Great Britain.

Manufacturing is an important industry. Lighting products, radio and television equipment, computer parts, machine tools, and medical instruments are made there. The state produces a lot of leather, much of which goes to make shoes.

Forests cover over 80 percent of the land. Much of the timber is used in making paper products. Many fir trees are cut down for sale as Christmas trees each year.

Dairy products are important to the state. Farmers raise poultry and beef cattle. Apples, blueberries, strawberries, and grapes are also grown there.

New Hampshire produces maple sugar, mica, and granite. Many important buildings have been made from the state's granite including the Library of Congress in Washington, D.C.

Cool summers and snowy winters make the state a great tourist attraction for hiking, swimming, fishing, and snow skiing.

The coastline is only 17 miles long, shorter than any other state bordering an ocean. The mountains are higher than any in the Northeast.

**Entered union:** June 21, 1788
                (9th state)
**Motto:** Live free or die
**Square miles:** 9,304
**Abbreviations:** N.H. (traditional)
                       NH (postal)

**State bird:** purple finch           **State tree:** paper birch
**State flower:** purple lilac

**Flag:** blue, with the state seal in the middle

# NEW JERSEY

**Capital:** Trenton

**State name:** named after the island of Jersey south of England.

**Nickname:** The Garden State

## Facts About New Jersey

The Dutch were the first settlers in New Jersey in the early 1600s. The state was one of the original 13 colonies. About 100 Revolutionary War battles were fought there, including the Battle of Trenton, where Washington crossed the Delaware River. Both Princeton and Trenton served temporarily as the nation's capital in the 1780s.

New Jersey is the home of many firsts. Edison invented the electric light, movie camera, and record player there. Morse invented the telegraph. Other firsts were the submarine, steam engine, balloon flight, drive-in movie, and baseball game.

New Jersey is one of the major manufacturing states. It is first in the production of drugs. Chemicals, food products, and machines such as radios, televisions, washing machines, and stoves are made there.

Transportation and communications equipment and glass-making are other big industries.

A wide variety of crops such as tomatoes, blueberries, cranberries, and roses are grown.

The New Jersey coast on the Atlantic Ocean is popular with tourists. Among the many resorts is Atlantic City, which features the Boardwalk and the Miss America pageant.

The land is mostly plains with mountains in the northwest.

**Entered union:** December 18, 1787
(3rd state)

**Motto:** Liberty and prosperity

**Square miles:** 7,836

**Abbreviations:** N.J. (traditional)
NJ (postal)

  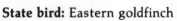

**State bird:** Eastern goldfinch          **State tree:** Northern red oak
**State flower:** purple violet

**Flag:** the state seal on a
tan background

# NEW MEXICO

**Capital:** Santa Fe

**State name:** Spanish for "area."

**Nickname:** Land of Enchantment

## Facts About New Mexico

New Mexico is a combination of both old and new lifestyles. There are old Spanish villages, Indian pueblos, and prehistoric Indian ruins next to shopping centers and airports. There are 22 Indian reservations; the Navajo reservation is the largest in the country.

Mining is a major source of income. The state ranks first in potash, a mineral used in fertilizer, and uranium, which is used for nuclear power.

Agriculture, especially cattle and sheep ranching, is important. Because the land is so dry, much of it is irrigated. Some crops grown are cotton, chile, wheat, onions, and pecans.

Tourists come to New Mexico because of the pleasant climate, historical sites, and outdoor activities such as skiing and fishing. Carlsbad Caverns, the largest connected group of underground caves ever discovered, is popular.

The first atomic bomb was built and exploded in the state in 1945. New Mexico is still a major center for rocket and nuclear energy research.

New Mexico is a scenic state, with the Rocky Mountains in the center, deserts in the south, and plains in the east.

**Entered union:** January 6, 1912
(47th state)

**Motto:** *Crescit eundo*
(It grows as it goes)

**Square miles:** 121,666

**Abbreviations:** N.M. (traditional)
NM (postal)

**State bird:** roadrunner

**State flower:** yucca flower

**State tree:** piñon

**Flag:** yellow with an
ancient sun symbol in red

# NEW YORK

**Capital:** Albany

**State name:** named for the Duke of York

**Nickname:** Empire State

## Facts About New York

The Dutch established the first settlement in New York at what is now Albany in 1624. Forty years later, the English took control of the area. Over one-third of the Revolutionary War battles were fought there. In the beginning of this century, many people from faraway lands immigrated to New York City.

The state is the home of part of Niagara Falls; the Erie Canal, which connects Lake Erie and the Hudson River; and the U.S. Military Academy at West Point.

New York City is the largest city in the United States. It is a leading banking, trade, and cultural center. George Washington was inaugurated there when it was the nation's first capital. The Statue of Liberty, the Empire State Building, the United Nations, and many theaters and museums are located there.

Manufacturing is one of the state's main industries. It ranks first in printing and publishing, photographic equipment, and clothing.

New York is a leading dairy state. Some crops grown are beets, cabbage, apples, and grapes. Maple syrup is produced there.

The Adirondack Mountains are in northern New York and the Catskills are in the south. The rest of the land is mostly lakes, valleys, and hills.

Entered union: July 26, 1788
(11th state)

Motto: *Excelsior*
(Ever upward)

Square miles: 49,576

Abbreviations: N.Y. (traditional)
NY (postal)

State bird: bluebird

State flower: rose

State tree: sugar maple

Flag: blue, with the state seal in the middle

# NORTH CAROLINA

**Capital:** Raleigh

**State name:** comes from "Carolana," which means "Land of Charles" (named for King Charles I of England).

**Nickname:** The Tar Heel State

## Facts About North Carolina

North Carolina was the site of the second English settlement in America, later known as "The Lost Colony." Virginia Dare, the first child of English parents to be born in America, was born there.

The first airplane flight (the Wright Brothers) took place at Kitty Hawk on December 17, 1903.

The first operating silver mine in the U.S. opened near Lexington in 1838. It is now closed.

Manufacturing is the main industry. The state leads the nation in the production of tobacco products, textiles, wooden furniture, and bricks. Chemicals, paper, and electrical equipment are other important products.

Farming is also important. The leading crops are tobacco, corn, soybeans, and peanuts. Farmers also raise chickens, turkeys, and pigs.

The state attracts a lot of tourists. It is known as "Variety Vacationland" because it has both beautiful mountains and beaches. There are also swamps, hills, and forests. Mount Mitchell is the highest peak in the eastern United States.

**Entered union:** November 21, 1789
(12th state)

**Motto:** *Esse quam videri*
(To be rather than to seem)

**Square miles:** 52,586

**Abbreviations:** N.C. (traditional)
NC (postal)

**State bird:** cardinal

**State tree:** pine

**State flower:** dogwood

**Flag:** red, white, and blue, with the dates of the two North Carolina declarations of independence printed on the left

# NORTH DAKOTA

**Capital:** Bismarck

**State name:** comes from the Sioux Indians, who called themselves "Dakota," which means "friends."

**Nickname:** The Flickertail State

## Facts About North Dakota

Indians have lived in North Dakota for centuries. Today, there are still several Indian reservations. The North Dakota area was claimed for France by La Salle in 1682 and was later sold to the United States as part of the Louisiana Purchase. Lewis and Clark explored the area in the early 1800s.

Agriculture is a big industry. Farmers raise sunflowers, barley, rye, flaxseed (used in making linseed oil), durum wheat (used in making pasta), hard red spring wheat (used in making bread), corn, sugar beets, and potatoes.

Food processing is a big manufacturing activity. This includes butter, cheddar cheese, honey, and sugar. Farm equipment production is also important.

Tourists who visit North Dakota can see what the Old West was like. Rodeos and Indian ceremonies are popular. People also visit the International Peace Garden on the U.S.-Canadian border, Theodore Roosevelt National Park, and historical buildings such as Fort Lincoln which was General Custer's headquarters.

Plains and prairies cover most of the land. The Red River forms the eastern border. Part of Canada is the northern border. The Missouri River flows through the state.

**Entered union:** November 2, 1889
(39th state)

**Motto:** Liberty and union, now and forever,
one and inseparable

**Square miles:** 70,665

**Abbreviations:** N.D. (traditional)
ND (postal)

**State bird:** western meadowlark

**State tree:** American elm

**State flower:** wild prairie rose

**Flag:** the coat of arms on
a blue background

# OHIO

**Capital:** Columbus

**State name:** comes from the Iroquois Indian word meaning "something great."

**Nickname:** The Buckeye State

## Facts About Ohio

Indians called Mound Builders lived in Ohio many years ago. They are known for their burial mounds and forts that can still be seen today. La Salle explored the area in the late 1600s, and George Washington toured the Ohio River Valley in 1752. The first settlement, Marietta, was founded by Revolutionary War veterans who were offered land as payment for serving in the war.

The first major league baseball team, cash register, school safety patrol, chewing gum, and kindergarten came from or were started in Ohio.

Ohio is one of the leading manufacturing states. Products made there include glassware, machine tools, soap, baseballs, transportation equipment such as truck and bus bodies, rubber products such as tires, farm machinery, coal, and paper.

Dairy products and eggs are big in the state. Farmers raise hay, soybeans, wheat, corn, tobacco, hogs, and beef cattle.

The Ohio River forms the southern border and Lake Erie is on the north. The land is mostly rolling hills with lakes and rivers.

Entered union: March 1, 1803
(17th state)

Motto: With God, all things are possible

Square miles: 41,222

Abbreviation: OH

State bird: cardinal

State tree: Ohio buckeye

State flower: scarlet carnation

Flag: pennant-shaped, with red and white stripes, and a blue area on the left

# OKLAHOMA

**Capital:** Oklahoma City

**State name:** a combination of two Choctaw Indian words meaning "red" and "people."

**Nickname:** The Sooner State

## Facts About Oklahoma

Indians played a major part in Oklahoma's history. The United States bought most of the state as part of the Louisiana Purchase in 1803. Much of the land was made into Indian reservations. This was referred to as Indian Territory. Indians from all over the country were brought there to live. Today, Oklahoma has the second largest Indian population in the U.S. and has more Indian tribes than any state.

The first flowing commercial oil well, Boy Scout troop, passenger plane, rolling supermarket cart, and parking meter were in or from Oklahoma.

The discovery of oil in the early part of this century brought many people to the area. There are oil derricks on the Capitol grounds in Oklahoma City.

Making oil field machinery and equipment is a big industry. Cars, window glass, and aircraft are also made there.

Farmers raise wheat, livestock, peanuts, cotton, pecans, and soybeans.

Tourists come to Oklahoma to see Old West events such as rodeos and Indian pow-wows.

The land is mostly hills, mountains, plains, forests, and mesas.

**Entered union:** November 16, 1907
(46th state)

**Motto:** *Labor omnia vincit*
(Labor conquers all things)

**Square miles:** 69,919

**Abbreviations:** Okla. (traditional)
OK (postal)

**State bird:** scissor-tailed flycatcher          **State tree:** Eastern redbud
**State flower:** mistletoe

**Flag:** an Osage warrior's shield in a field of blue with the shield crossed by a peace pipe and olive branch

# OREGON

**Capital:** Salem

**State name:** some say it was taken from the writings of Major Robert Rogers, an English army officer.

**Nickname:** The Beaver State

## Facts About Oregon

Lewis and Clark ended their exploration of the U.S. in Oregon in 1805. They built Fort Clatsup on the Columbia River. In 1850, the government passed a law that gave free land to settlers. Many came to the state on the rugged Oregon Trail.

Oregon is a leading timber state. Its many sawmills and lumber mills make plywood, lumber, paper, and other wood products.

Recreational and commercial fishing for salmon, shrimp, and crab is a big business.

Canning and freezing of fruits, vegetables and fish make food processing an important industry.

Agriculture is also important. Growing wheat and raising cattle are two major activities. Farmers also grow barley, oats, flower bulbs, grass seed, cherries, and peaches.

Oregon is known for its scenic beauty. Tourism is a leading industry. The Pacific Ocean, the state's western border, has beaches and steep cliffs. The Cascade Mountains offer many skiing and camping areas. Crater Lake, in Crater Lake National Park, is the deepest lake in the United States.

**Entered union:** February 14, 1859
(33rd state)
**Motto:** The Union
**Square miles:** 96,981
**Abbreviations:** Ore. (traditional),
OR (postal)

**State bird:** Western meadowlark  **State tree:** Douglas fir
**State flower:** Oregon grape

**Flag:** blue, with the state
seal

# PENNSYLVANIA

**Capital:** Harrisburg

**State name:** means "Penn's woods," from William Penn, a Quaker who started a colony.

**Nickname:** The Keystone State

## Facts About Pennsylvania

Pennsylvania was one of the original 13 colonies. The state played an important part in colonial America. Many Revolutionary War battles were fought there and Philadelphia was the U.S. capital for a while.

The production of pig iron, steel, and hard coal is a major industry.

Manufacturing is also important. Metal products, machinery, food products, and textiles are all made there.

The state is a leader in the production of mushrooms, cigar leaf tobacco, pretzels, sausage products, and potato chips.

Tourism is a big industry. People come to visit such sites as Hershey, which has the largest chocolate factory in the world. The Liberty Bell, Independence Hall, and Ben Franklin's print shop, located in Philadelphia, are also popular. Valley Forge and Gettysburg are also in the state.

Many Pennsylvania Dutch, who live and dress as their German ancestors did, live in southeast Pennsylvania.

The land is mostly hills, plateaus, and valleys. Forests cover part of the state. The northwestern corner borders on Lake Erie.

Entered union: December 12, 1787
(2nd state)

Motto: Virtue, liberty, and independence

Square miles: 45,333

Abbreviations: Pa. (traditional)
PA (postal)

**State bird:** ruffed grouse          **State tree:** Eastern hemlock

**State flower:** mountain laurel

**Flag:** blue, with the state
coat of arms

# RHODE ISLAND

**Capital:** Providence

**State name:** officially it is "Rhode Island and Providence Plantations."

**Nickname:** The Ocean State

## Facts About Rhode Island

Rhode Island was one of the original 13 colonies and the first to declare its independence from England. The first settlers came from Massachusetts in 1636. They were searching for political and religious freedom, which the Massachusetts government would not give them.

The first U.S. textile mill, synagogue, dry goods store, and torpedo boat were built in Rhode Island.

Manufacturing is the leading industry. Jewelry, silverware, textiles, and boats are some of the products.

Fishing for tuna, swordfish, and shellfish (lobsters and clams) is important.

Dairy products such as butter, cheese, and eggs are important income sources. Farmers also grow apples and peaches.

Rhode Island is a popular summer resort area. Water sports such as fishing and sailing are popular. Newport, on the Atlantic Ocean, is famous for its large mansions built in the late 1800s.

Rhode Island is only 37 miles wide and 48 miles long, making it the smallest state. Narragansett Bay divides the state.

Entered union: May 29, 1790
            (13th state)
Motto: Hope
Square miles: 1,214
Abbreviations: R.I. (traditional)
               RI (postal)

State bird: Rhode Island Red chicken
State flower: violet

State tree: red maple

Flag: 13 gold stars on a
white background

# SOUTH CAROLINA

**Capital:** Columbia

**State name:** named for King Charles I. "Carolina" is a Latin form for Charles.

**Nickname:** The Palmetto State

## Facts About South Carolina

South Carolina played a big part in the Civil War. It was the first state to secede (break away) from the United States. Many Revolutionary and Civil War battles were fought there. The Civil War began at Fort Sumter on April 12, 1861.

The Charleston Museum is the oldest in the nation.

Many people work in the textile industry. The state ranks high in the making of textiles and the number of textile machines. Chemical production is another important industry.

Agriculture is a big industry. Farmers raise tobacco, soybeans, tomatoes, cucumbers, watermelons, peaches, kiwi fruit, tea, and beef. They also produce pork products and eggs.

The tourist business is important. Charleston and the beaches along the coast are popular places. People also come to see the beautiful buildings and plantations built before the Civil War.

The eastern part of the state borders the Atlantic Ocean. There are also hills, mountains, forests, plains, and rivers.

**Entered union:** May 23, 1788
  (8th state)

**Motto:** *Dum spiro spero*
  (While I breathe, I hope)

**Square miles:** 31,055

**Abbreviations:** S.C. (traditional)
  SC (postal)

**State bird:** Carolina wren          **State tree:** cabbage palmetto
          **State flower:** yellow jessamine

**Flag:** blue, with a white palmetto tree and a white quarter moon

# SOUTH DAKOTA

**Capital:** Pierre

**State name:** comes from the Sioux Indians who called themselves "Dakota," which means "friends."

**Nickname:** The Sunshine State

## Facts About South Dakota

Indians lived in the South Dakota area as far back as 5000 B.C. The first permanent settlement, Fort Pierre, was built in 1817. Battles between Indians and U.S. troops took place in the 1800s.

Agriculture is the leading industry. Cattle, sheep, and hogs are raised. Farmers also grow wheat, potatoes, corn, oats, and sunflowers.

The discovery of gold by General Custer's troops in 1874 created a gold rush that brought many people to the area. Today, the state ranks first in gold production. Homestake Mine, in the town of Lead, is the largest gold-producing mine in the United States.

Tourism is important. People come to see rodeos and Indian ceremonies. Mount Rushmore in the Black Hills is the world's largest man-made sculpture. Badlands National Park is another popular tourist spot.

South Dakota is known for its different land regions. The Missouri River divides the state in half. East of the river, the land is mostly farmland. To the west, the land is mostly prairies and mountains. This includes the Black Hills, named for the black-green ponderosa pines. In the southwest are the Badlands, which are deep gorges and bare hills.

**Entered union:** November 2, 1889
(40th state)

**Motto:** Under God the people rule

**Square miles:** 77,047

**Abbreviations:** S.D. (traditional)
SD (postal)

**State bird:** ring-necked pheasant          **State tree:** white spruce
**State flower:** pasqueflower

**Flag:** the state seal on a
blue background

# TENNESSEE

**Capital:** Nashville

**State name:** comes from "Tanasie," the name of a Cherokee village in the area.

**Nickname:** The Volunteer State

## Facts About Tennessee

Indians lived in Tennessee's mountains and forests. Pioneers settled in the area in the 1700s. The state played a major part in the Civil War. It was the last Confederate state to leave the Union and the first to rejoin. Many Civil War battles, including Shiloh and Chickamauga, were fought there.

Farmers grow soybeans, tobacco, corn, and cotton.

Manufacturing is a major industry. Some products include fabricated metals, wood products, clothing, bathroom fixtures, fireplugs, cars, and saddles.

Printing and publishing are also important, as is coal mining.

Tennessee is the only state to have a horse named after it — the Tennessee Walking Horse.

During World War II, the atomic bomb was partly developed at Oak Ridge.

Tourists come to visit the Grand Ole Opry near Nashville and Great Smoky Mountain National Park.

There are mountains in the east and plains in the west. There are also forests, rivers, and waterfalls. The Mississippi River is the western border.

**Entered union:** June 1, 1796
                  (16th state)
**Motto:** Agriculture and commerce
**Square miles:** 42,244
**Abbreviations:** Tenn. (traditional)
                  TN (postal)

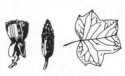

**State bird:** mockingbird

**State flower:** iris

**State tree:** yellow poplar

**Flag:** red with white stars
on a blue background

# TEXAS

**Capital:** Austin

**State name:** from "tejas," an Indian word meaning "friendly."

**Nickname:** The Lone Star State

## Facts About Texas

Texas was a part of Mexico until 1836 when Sam Houston and his men fought for independence in the Battle of San Jacinto. The area was an independent republic until 1845 when it became a state.

The largest state capitol building in the country is in Austin.

Texas ranks first among the states in the production of oil, natural gas, and chemicals made from petroleum.

More cotton is grown there than in any state. Farmers also raise cabbage, spinach, watermelons, sorghum, pecans, and cattle.

Tourists visiting Texas can see big, modern cities such as Houston and Dallas. They can also see places and events from the past such as rodeos and the Alamo. Other popular attractions include the Johnson Space Center, Big Bend National Park, and the Astrodome.

Texas is a very large state. An old Texas jingle is "The sun is riz, the sun is set, and we ain't out of Texas yet." The land is mostly plains with mountains in the west. The Gulf of Mexico is part of the eastern border. Mexico is its neighbor to the south.

**Entered union:** December 29, 1845
(28th state)

**Motto:** Friendship

**Square miles:** 267,338

**Abbreviations:** Tex. (traditional)
TX (postal)

**State bird:** mockingbird

**State flower:** bluebonnet

**State tree:** pecan

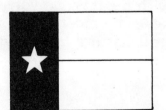

**Flag:** red, white, and blue

# UTAH

**Capital:** Salt Lake City

**State name:** named after the Ute Indians who lived there.

**Nickname:** The Beehive State

## Facts About Utah

Indian ruins from as long as 10,000 years ago have been found in Utah. Spanish missionaries were the first explorers. In 1847, a religious group of people from Illinois called Mormons made the first settlement. They built communities and irrigated the land. Today, Salt Lake City is the center of the Mormons, known now as the Church of Jesus Christ of Latter Day Saints. The Mormon Tabernacle Choir is located there.

Tourism is a big industry. People come to ski and visit the beautiful national parks.

Missile production, metal fabricating, high technology, and steel and pipe production are important.

Utah is one of the top mining states. Copper is the leading mineral. Gold, silver, petroleum, and coal are also mined.

Much of the land is irrigated so farmers can grow hay, fruit, wheat, and melons. Livestock, turkeys, and dairy products are also important.

Utah is a beautiful state with deserts, canyons, rivers, mountains, plateaus, and lakes. The most famous lake is the Great Salt Lake, the largest natural lake west of the Mississippi. It is saltier than the ocean.

Entered union: January 4, 1896
(45th state)

Motto: Industry

Square miles: 84,916

Abbreviation: UT

State bird: seagull

State flower: sego lily

State tree: blue spruce

Flag: the state seal on a blue background

# VERMONT

**Capital:** Montpelier

**State name:** comes from the French words "vert mont," which mean "green mountain."

**Nickname:** The Green Mountain State

## Facts About Vermont

Vermont was claimed for France by Champlain in 1609. During the French and Indian War, England took the area away from France. Though Vermont was not a colony during the Revolutionary War, it fought with the Colonists. Ethan Allen and the Green Mountain Boys took Fort Ticonderoga from the British in one battle. After the Revolutionary War, Vermont was the first state to join the original 13 states.

America's first electric motor, canal, ski lift, steel plow, and marble quarry came from or operated in Vermont.

Manufacturing is the leading industry. Machine tools, wood products, computer parts, and pipe organs are made there. Processing granite and marble is also important.

Vermont's big dairy industry produces eggs, cheese, and milk. Many maple products such as maple syrup are made in the state.

Comfortable summers, colorful autumn leaves, and winter sports make Vermont a popular tourist area. The small New England towns, historical sites, and covered wooden bridges also attract visitors.

Canada borders on the north and the Connecticut River borders on the east. Lake Champlain is on the west. The land features lakes, valleys, rivers, forests, and rolling mountains.

Entered union: March 4, 1791
(14th state)

Motto: Vermont, freedom, and unity

Square miles: 9,609

Abbreviations: Vt. (traditional),
VT (postal)

State bird: hermit thrush          State tree: sugar maple
State flower: red clover

Flag: the coat of arms on
a blue background

# VIRGINIA

**Capital:** Richmond

**State name:** named after Queen Elizabeth I of England, the Virgin Queen.

**Nickname:** The Old Dominion

## Facts About Virginia

Jamestown, founded in 1607, was the first permanent English settlement in the U.S. Both the Revolutionary and Civil Wars were surrendered in Virginia. Eight U.S. presidents were born there.

Manufacturing is the state's leading industry. Products include chemicals, textiles, cigarettes, and paper products.

Farmers raise apples, peanuts, tobacco, turkeys, and chickens. Dairy farming is important.

Virginia is famous for its Smithfield hams made from peanut-fed hogs.

Coal mining is an important industry.

Virginia is a big fishing state. Catches include oysters, crabs, bass, and flounder.

Tourists like to visit the historic sites such as Williamsburg, Mount Vernon, Monticello, Yorktown, and Arlington National Cemetery. The beaches are popular in the summer. Chincoteague Island is famous for its wild ponies.

There are mountains and valleys in the west. The Atlantic Ocean and Chesapeake Bay are the eastern border.

**Entered union:** June 25, 1788
(10th state)

**Motto:** *Sic semper tyrannis*
(Thus always to tyrants)

**Square miles:** 40,817

**Abbreviations:** Va. (traditional)
VA (postal)

**State bird:** cardinal

**State flower:** dogwood

**State tree:** flowering dogwood

**Flag:** the state seal on a
blue background

# WASHINGTON

**Capital:** Olympia

**State name:** named after George Washington

**Nickname:** The Evergreen State

## Facts About Washington

The first explorers in Washington were probably the Spanish and English sailing along the coast in the 1500s. Russian, English, and American fur trappers and traders set up trading posts in the 1700s. Lewis and Clark explored Washington in 1805. The Alaska Gold Rush of 1879 brought many people to the area.

The manufacturing of aircraft equipment is a leading industry. Canning and preserving fish are also important.

Washington is a big lumber state. Its many forests provide wood for lumber products such as paper.

Farmers grow a variety of crops, including winter wheat, potatoes, cherries, hay, asparagus, and strawberries. The state ranks first in apples.

Fishing for salmon is a popular sport.

Washington is a scenic state with the Cascade Mountains dividing the state in half. The Pacific Ocean forms the western border; Canada is on the north. The land is mostly mountains and forests in the west and farmland in the east. Mount St. Helens, which erupted in 1980, is a famous volcano.

**Entered union:** November 11, 1889
(42nd state)

**Motto:** *Alki*
(By and by)

**Square miles:** 68,192

**Abbreviations:** Wash. (traditional)
WA (postal)

**State bird:** willow goldfinch          **State tree:** Western hemlock
**State flower:** coast rhododendron

**Flag:** the state seal on a
green background

# WEST VIRGINIA

**Capital:** Charleston

**State name:** was named after it separated from Virginia during the Civil War.

**Nickname:** The Mountain State

## Facts About West Virginia

Indians lived in the area as early as 3000 B.C. New Mecklenburg, one of the first settlements, was founded by Germans who came from Pennsylvania seeking religious freedom. West Virginia was part of Virginia until the Civil War. The two states separated when West Virginia refused to side with the Confederacy.

The state was the home of the first steamboat, brick street, and rural-route delivery. One of the first Revolutionary War battles was fought at Pleasant Point. The first Mother's Day was held at Grafton in 1908.

Petroleum, coal, gas, stone, sand, gravel, and clay are mined. Producing steel and chemicals are also important. Plastics, fabrics, and glass products such as marbles and car windows are made there.

The timber industry is important. A lot of wood furniture is made there.

Farmers raise apples, peaches, and chickens.

The state is popular for hiking, white-water rafting, skiing, and mountain climbing. Tourists also come to buy the arts and crafts made by people living in the mountains.

The Appalachian Mountains make West Virginia a rugged state. Very little of the land is flat. There are also hills, rivers, and caverns.

Entered union: June 20, 1863
(35th state)

Motto: *Montani semper liberi*
(Mountaineers are always free)

Square miles: 24,181

Abbreviations: W.Va. (traditional)
WV (postal)

**State bird:** cardinal
**State flower:** rhododendron
**State tree:** sugar maple

**Flag:** the state seal on a white background

# WISCONSIN

**Capital:** Madison

**State name:** named after the Wisconsin River, which flows through the center of the state.

**Nickname:** The Badger State

## Facts About Wisconsin

In 1634, Jean Nicolet of France became the first person to explore Wisconsin. Marquette and Joliet later explored the area in the late 1600s.

The nation's first kindergarten, typewriter, hydroelectric plant, electric street car, snowmobile, ice cream sundae, malted milk, and Ringling Brothers Circus were from Wisconsin.

Agriculture is a leading industry. The state leads the nation in the production of milk products. It produces a lot of cheese, butter, beets, green peas, snap beans, hay, corn, and oats.

Manufacturing is also important. The state makes a lot of engines, farm machinery, paper, and construction equipment.

Canning peas, sweet corn, and other vegetables is a big business.

Tourists come for winter sports.

The state was mostly covered by glaciers about 25 million years ago. They left behind low hills, valleys, and many lakes. There are also thick forests.

**Entered union:** May 29, 1848
(30th state)

**Motto:** Forward

**Square miles:** 56,154

**Abbreviations:** Wisc. (traditional)
WI (postal)

**State bird:** robin

**State flower:** violet

**State tree:** sugar maple

**Flag:** blue with the state seal in the center

# WYOMING

**Capital:** Cheyenne

**State name:** comes from Indian word meaning "upon the great plain."

**Nickname:** The Equality State

## Facts About Wyoming

Indians were attracted to Wyoming by the many buffalo that roamed the area. The first settlement was Fort Bridger, a fur-trading post. It later served to protect settlers and travelers from Indian attacks. Today, the state has one Indian reservation.

The first national park (Yellowstone), national monument (Devil's Tower), and national forest (Shoshone) are in Wyoming.

Wyoming is an important mining state. Uranium, coal, gas, oil, iron, bentonite, and soda ash are found there.

Raising cattle and sheep is the biggest agricultural activity. Farmers also grow sugar beets, hay, barley, winter wheat, oats, dry beans, and potatoes.

Food processing, including sugar, cheese, meat, and honey, is a big industry.

Tourists come to visit Yellowstone and Grand Teton national parks. Old Faithful Geyser is a favorite site. Old West events such as rodeos and Indian ceremonies are also popular.

Parts of both the Great Plains and Rocky Mountains are in Wyoming. The land also has deserts, rolling grassland, lakes, and rivers.

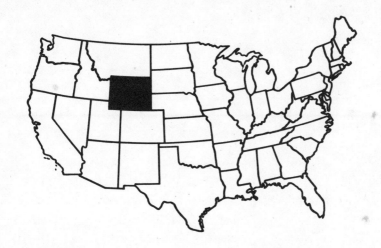

**Entered union:** July 10, 1890
(44th state)
**Motto:** Equal rights
**Square miles:** 97,914
**Abbreviations:** Wyo. (traditional)
WY (postal)

**State bird:** meadowlark
**State flower:** Indian paintbrush
**State tree:** plains cottonwood

**Flag:** the state seal on a buffalo, with a blue background and red border